Kemetic Karest mas Celebration & Education

Dr Terri Nelson aka Nteri Renenet Elson
Revealing the Harvest of the Neteru to the Sons and Daughters of God

This work is a synopsis, derivative, expansion and further clarification of earlier copyrighted and more comprehensive works titled, *Ka Ab Ba Buiding The Lighted Temple; MerKaBa:The Great Pyramid is the Tree of Life:KaAbBa, and Ausar Pope.*
Copyright © 2000, 2003, 2005, 2008, 2009, 2011, 2018. Dr Terri Nelson. Library of Congress Cataloging in Publication.

The press of Spirit causes this work to go forward now, even though it is still a work in process.

First Edition, Second Edition
Copyright © 2013. Dr Terri Nelson.
Third Edition, Second Edition
Copyright © 2018. Dr Terri Nelson.

Library of Congress Cataloging in Publication.
All Rights Reserved. No part of this book may be used or reproduced in any manner whatsoever without written permission except in the case of brief quotations embodied in critical articles and reviews. All inquiries may be forwarded to the address on the page that follows:

ISBN: 09659600-2-1
Printed in the United States of America
Published by:

Kemetic Karest mas Celebration & Education

The Academy of Kemetic Education & Wellness, Inc. Right Relationship Right Knowledge
53 Cedar St. Mattapan, MA 02126
Editor's Review: Adisa Makalani, Editor, Classic Transcripts
Dr. Nteri Nelson has once again engaged Maat by expanding our cultural vision. Just as Dr. Maulana Karenga took a giant step 47 years ago with the introduction of Kwanzaa, Dr. Nelson reaches back in the spirit of Sankofa to our Nilotic beginnings.

It is important to add this holy day to our cultural pantheon for a number of reasons. One: Every culture on the globe celebrates the astronomical event of the sun beginning its ascent to the equator after reaching its nadir. Two: The civilization that rose along the banks of the Nile is the mother and father all of civilizations; therefore to draw from that tradition is the most of sacred of all. Doesn't it say in somebody's holy book that you should honor your mother and father so that your days upon the earth may be long? What greater honor to your foremothers and forefather can you provide them than recovering their cultural birthright?

As Afrikan people we have much to recover. Professor John Henrik Clarke used to say; the best way to begin tomorrow's work is to start today.
Thank you Dr. Nteri for starting today!

This book is dedicated to – AMEN AMENET Infinite, eternal All in All, Neter, Neteru, Fount of All Possibility, Spirit that reveals to me.

The author is available for group lectures and individual consultations. For further information or to order additional copies contact:

AЖademy_{of}Kemetic Education&Wellness, INC.
Right Relationship and Right Knowledge
Afrikan Origin of The Ancient/Egyptian Wisdom
Awakening Жonsciousness
AЖE   Afrikan Жnowledge
Wsir/Ausarian Enlightenment
The Knowledge & Education That Awakens
1st Eye Awareness into
The Metaphysics, Art & Science of Daily Living
Leading to
Spiritual Transformation, Right Relationship,
Soul Purpose Living, & Service
Classes Held at:
53 Cedar St.   Mattapan MA 02126
www.rrrk.net   (617) 296 -7797

Kemetic Karest mas Celebration & Education

About the Author:
Terri Nelson, PhD.E, LICSW, MSW, MSEP, Shækem RA АЖЕ (Reiki) Master
aka Nteri Renenet Elson
The Neteru revealing Harvest to the Sons and Daughters of God
Dr. Nteri is a Metaphysician, Teacher of the Afrikan origins of the Ancient wisdom and a Holistic Psychotherapist. She has served as adjunct Professor in Afrikana studies at the University of Massachusetts in Boston. She is co-founder of, *The Academy of Kemetic Education & Wellness, Right Relationship Right Knowledge, Inc.* where she teaches an Afrikan Centered Model for Psychological, Spiritual and Character development, which is underpinned by the History of Ancient Afrika/Kemet (Egypt) and the Diaspora as a way of Self knowledge, healing and health.

As a Licensed Clinician, she has worked in the Behavioral/Mental Health field for the last 30 years providing counseling and consultation to individuals, couples, families, groups and agencies. She is an Independent Researcher, a gifted Symbologist and is a Student and Teacher of the language, Metu Neter (later called Hieroglyphics by the Greeks).

Her analysis and synthesis within psychological, historical, social, behavioral and metaphysical fields gives deep and penetrative insight into the journey of unfolding consciousness within the human family.

Dr Nteri is author of: *Ka Ab Ba Building The Lighted Temple; KaAbBa:The Great Pyramid is the Tree of Life:MerKaBa; Secrets of Race and Consciousness; Afrikan Cosmology Kemet: The Golden Sun Egg Uncracked; Ausar, The Pope, Santa Claus, Christmas, and Christianity; The Ausarian Dramatization of The Story of The Tree of Life Key. On The Way To Finding Your Soulmate; The Right Relationship Workbook and The Forgiveness Process Workbook.*

She has lectured at numerous conferences nationally and internationally which include: the Association for the Study of Classical Afrikan Civilization (ASCAC); Indigenous Afrikan Healers; First World Alliance; Institute for the Study of Race and Culture; The Nile Valley; Melanin; Sankofa; and Metu Neter; Diopian Institute for Scholarly Advancement Conferences, just to name a few. She has served as the Massachusetts Region Representative and Chairperson of the Spiritual Development Committee for ASCAC Eastern Region.

Kemetic Karest mas Celebration & Education

Table of Contents:

Chapter 1..10-16
- Why a Karest-mas Celebration of Kemet
Ka rest Mas Medu Neter Meaning.

Chapter 2..17-68
- Steps of Reclaiming and Incorporating Symbols in a Kemetic Karest mas Celebration & Education
  - Divine Trinity, Ausar, Auset, Heru..............18-19
  - African Madona and Child........................20-21
  - Ausar Neb Lord of the World.....................22-23
  - Metu Neter Ka Ab Ba..............................24-25
  - Aspects of Divinity..............................26-27
  - Tree of Life Building The Lighted Temple....28-29
  - Maat 42 Laws.....................................30-33
  - Judgement Scene, Amenta, Weigh, Heart......34-37
  - Ausar and sarcophagus............................38-39
  - Tamarisk Tree, Djed Pillar.......................40-41
  - 7 Soul Bodies, Planes of Consciousness........42-43
  - The Paut Neteru Tree of Life Linearly..........44-45
  - MerKaBa Luminous Energy Body Light......46-49
  Resurrection of the Sun - Son/Daughter,
  The Karest, Amsu Heru, 5 pointed, Star........50-53
  - Red and White Crown, Santa Hat...............54-57
  - Crook, Candy Cane................................58-59
  - Djed/Tet Pillar Tamarisk, Evergreen Tree.....60-63
  - Sledge and Sleigh................................64-65
  - Divine Presence Neb Ausar.......................66-68

Chapter 3..69-119

- **Steps of Preview and Actual Participation in a Kemetic Karest mas Celebration & Education**
- **Full Description, Directions, Diagrams**
- **Steps to Take in Advance 10a - k**

What you will want to/Prepare and have on hand in advance for your Celebration.................69-73
Steps 1 Floor/room plan, directions ……… ...…..74
Step 2 Facing East, Pour Libation to, Recitation from the Prt em Hru...................... ...….....75-77
Step 3 Facing West, Stand before Scales, The 42 Laws Maat….....................................….........77-78
Step 4a - c Facing South/North Lowering/Raising Djed Pillar, Tamarisk tree Pillar of Stability, Recitation from the Prt em Hru ………….......79-85
Step 5a Adorning the Evergreen Tamarisk Tree sphere for each Neteru/Lighting ....
Step 5b Order of Adorning......................….…85-87
Step 5c Recite the Qualities of each Neteru.. 88-99
Step 5d Completing the Adorning............100-101
Step 6 Facing North Recite Hymn To Heru 102-103
Step 7 Facing East, Shrine of Ausar, each family member, Law of Maat, Quality of the Neteru greater presence.........….................….......104-107
Step 8 Circling. Planes of Consciousness, Sing Re-ascension......................................108-110
Step 9 Feast with family and community….......111
Steps of Reclaiming and Incorporating
◦Imiut Symbol….....…................................112- 117
Step 10a What to have on hand...................118

8

Kemetic Karest mas Celebration & Education

Available at www.rrrk.net...............................119
Bibliography...........…............................…...120

Chapter 1

- The **Kemetic Karest mas Celebration & Education** is not to be confused with the Christmas Cele-bration.
- Like Kwanzaa demonstrates an Afrikan Celebration, this book demonstrates the practice of a Kemetically Conscious Karest mas Celebration by our Afrikan Ancestors of the Nile Valley, Kemet, the land of the Blacks, later called Egypt by the Greeks.
- In this reconstruction of a Kemetic Karest mas Celebration & Education our first step is to pull back the veil that has been thrown upon our Afrikan Spirituality.
- This, in order to re-Spiritualize those elements of our Traditional Afrikan Spirituality, symbols and ritual practices that have become, materialized, perverted, Europeanized, debased, re-named, and potentized to be injurious to the Afrikan consciousness. They have been 'dressed up' to appear familiar but strange, inviting yet detrimental.
- Just as if our own child were going out the door dressed with clothes strewn any old way, we would call them back and say, "You are not going out of the house looking that way." (i.e. in ways not natural, not Divine/Neter).
- Likewise we must call back, and declare, "Take that off," as we reclaim our sacred symbols and ritual practices, once the distortions are removed and

Kemetic Karest mas Celebration & Education

their meaning is ungarbled. The Steps in this book move us through the re-educating, reclaiming, ritualizing and incorporating of each symbol in a Kemetic Karest mas Celebration & Education.
• This research is based on the wisdom of our ancestors as recorded in the Pyramid Texts, The Prt em Hru and Metu Neter language and the books that I have authored and shown on the page that follows:
◦ *Ka Ab Ba BuildingThe Lighted Temple/ Metaphysical Keys Tree Life and*
◦ *KaAbBa: The Great Pyramid is The Tree of Life: MerKaBa*

One can learn more by referring to these foundational Texts that this present work is based.
• The Prt em Hru is a primary source text that reveals the evidences of a **Kemetic Karest mas** birth, death and resurrection, thousands of years before Christianity, the bible and the Christ. This text is later erroneously renamed, *The Egyptian Book Of The Dead,* by European so called Egyptologists, who through campaigns of Kemet invasions, seized and created a whole discipline for studying our Afrikan antiquities, and would become 'custodial' via acquisition by theft.

Ka Ab Ba Building The Lighted Temple/ Metaphysical Keys To The Tree Of Life

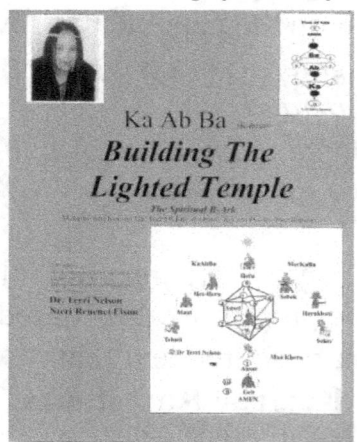

Afrikan Centered Psychology, Human/ Character/Consciousness Development, Spirituality, Historically Underpinned by Afrikan and Diaspora History

©Copyright Dr Nteri Nelson

MerKaBa: The Great Pyramid is The Tree Of Life: KaAbBa
Kemetic Technology For Remaking Ourselves as Beings of Light

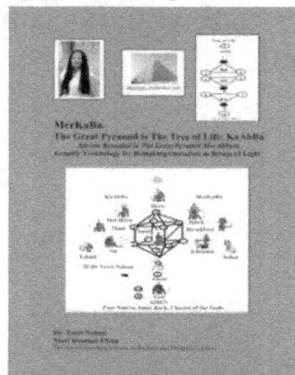

Kemetic Karest mas Celebration & Education

- This book serves as a guide for all ages and interest levels. It likewise suggests deeper study to every reader, of all that is presented within its 'two doors' or book covers. When enacted by you and community, at the appointed time:
- The Kemetic Karest mas Celebration, deeply profound in meaning and spiritually transformative, holds keys to the powerful *Reparation* and *Spiritual Prescription* we can give to ourselves now, having suffered the impact of Maafa (terrible occurrence) in our terrestrial Earthly journey into the 'Underworld' during our enslavement.
- Keys to cleansing, clearing, revitalizing, restoring, reclaimaing, re-Spiritualizing, resurrecting and returning again to our Mother land, after having gone out on, *The Spiritual Journey of Unfolding Consciousness.*
- In Chapter 1 the basics for restoring a Kemetic Karest mas Celebration & Education are given.
- In Chapter 2 you, your family and community are guided through Key Kemetic Symbols. Viewing, meditating upon, studying, researching, consciously reconnecting with and reclaiming 'each' one as your own, is recommended.
- In Chapter 3 you are walked through the Steps of performing the celebration. Things you will need to do in advance are explained. A list of things that you will need to have on hand as part of your celebration

and how you may obtain these is given. Please see our website www.rrrk.net.

• The Metu Neter language is later named Hieroglyphics by the Greeks, as has so much in our history.
• When we look at the Title: Karest mas we are brought to the Metu Neter terms given to us by our Afrikann ancestors who teach us that:
• Ka is Spirit, All is Spirit Ka.
Ka, Spirit takes of the substance of Itself to see Itself in form, to manifest.
• Karest is how we arise as we move in a continuous cycle of birth and rebirth, from the tomb to the womb, to be born again.

• Mas is birth.

It is the birth of an ever living and eternal Spirit that is taking place within us.
• Just as cosmically our Sun, undergoes a seeming death at the Winter Solstice only to be resurrected

Kemetic Karest mas Celebration & Education

again, so too, does man and woman, as son and daughter, enact a seeming death and rebirth or resurrection – as a Karest, the ever coming ONE, the Spirit that does not die, but is reborn.
This is expressed accordingly: Prt em Hru p. 247.
> The deceased is always identified with Ausar, or the sun which has set, the judge and god of the dead. As the sun sets in the west and rises again in the east, so the dead man is laid in his tomb on the western bank of the Nile, and after being acquitted in the Hall of Judgment, proceeds to the east to begin a new existence.

- The Kemetic Karest mas Celebration is held at the Winter Solstice on December 21 (or varying one to two days before or one to two days after) depending on the year. The Winter Solstice marks the point when our Sun, the Great Solar Neter, Ra, reaches its greatest descent in the sky, such that we experience the longest night and the shortest day in its yearly cycle.
- During this increase towards greatest darkness, a moment of descent is reached wherein the Sun seemingly 'stands still', undergoes a seeming death, then a rebirth and resurrection, as it again begins its gradual ascent in the sky and increase towards greatest light. (As light increases and The Sun reaches its greatest ascent in the sky we experience the longest day and the shortest night in the yearly cycle – the Summer Solstice June 21 or varying one to two days before or one to two days after).

- We suffer a seeming 'death' at the Winter Solstice, not from increasing drought, as in the Summer Solstice in Kemet, Afrika, but from increasing darkness. For our Afrikan Ancestors, drought and darkness are synonymous: The former overcome with the approaching heliacal rising of the star Sopdet, (called Sirius by the Greeks) heralding the flooding of the Nile River. The latter overcome by the flooding again of Solar Light of Ra.
- The specific energies of this time in the Winter Solstice cycle of our Sun and all its symbolism must be Kemetically understood and reclaimed for the resurrection of the mind, body and Soul of Afrikan people.
- Let us move through the Steps of reclaiming and incorporating each symbol in a Kemetic Karest mas Celebration

Kemetic Karest mas Celebration & Education

Chapter 2

As we move through the Step of reclaiming and incorporating each Symbol in a Kemetic Karest mas Celebration & Education allow your consciousness to be with each one, taking in, meditating upon, remembering, studying, researching, reconnecting, consciously reconnecting with and reclaiming 'each' Symbol, as your own, is recommended.

Symbol reclaimed and incorporated is:
- Divine Trinity, W/Ausar, Auset, Heru
- Later re-named Osiris, Isis, Horus by the Greeks.
- This Celestial and Terrestrial Afrikan Family Predates Christianity.
- The Divine Trinity of Ausar The Divine Father, Auset The Divine Mother and Heru The Divine Son-Daughter are within us.

Kemetic Karest mas Celebration & Education

The Divine Trinity

- Ausar
- Auset
- Heru

Symbol reclaimed and incorporated is:
- The Divine Mother. Afrikan Madonna and Child, Auset and Heru. Heru is the Karest, that is within us.
- Later, these symbols take on a different appearance and are named, Mary and Jesus the Christ.

Kemetic Karest mas Celebration & Education

Afrikan Madonna and Child
Auset and Heru

Symbol reclaimed and incorporated is:
- W/Ausar, Neb, Lord of the World

W/Ausar

Kemetic Karest mas Celebration & Education

●The symbol of Wsir or Ausar would later be Christianized as the Pope. The symbols of power of Ausar would also be Christianized.

Ausar and Pope

Symbol reclaimed and incorporated is:
- Ka Ab Ba, the sacred symbols and language of Metu Neter.
- These key terms, Ka Ab Ba, give us the wisdom for Building The Lighted Temple, the monument, which is us.
- The Pyramid text, the Prt em Hru, the Metu Neter, teach us that our Afrikan ancestors were Masters in the Science of the Soul, Journey of the Soul and the Spiritual Anatomy of our constitution, which is both human and divine. As previously discussed:
- **Ka** is Spirit. All is Spirit. The Ka symbol, with up stretched arms and in its 'double' aspect, is pictured on page that follows:

Ka above is Spirit, taking of the substance of Itself, to see itself in form, Ka below is Spirit in its physical-izing, manifestation, aspect.
- **Ab** for the Kemetians is symbolized by the human heart, shown here. Ab is the seat of conscience and growing soul consciousness. This is where we locate the Heru or Ka-rest within us.
- **Ba** means Soul, symbolized by a Hawk.

It is an individualization of
Spirit, Ka. As we become fully conscious of
the relationship between Spirit and Matter,
Heru within us, becomes the fully conscious Ba
 Soul or Ausar in his/her journey. Heru becomes as
Ausar. This is later reframed by Christianity as My Father and I are one, leaving the Mother out. As we

Kemetic Karest mas Celebration & Education

shall see, Ka and Ba, Mother and Father, Ausar and Auset are One.

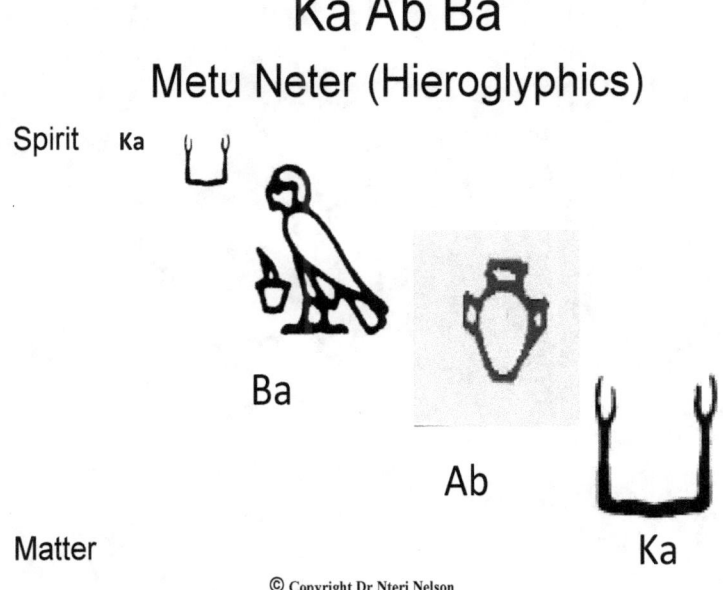

Symbol reclaimed and incorporated is:
- Ka Ab Ba corresponds with the Divine Trinity of Auset, Heru and Ausar, which are the 3 Aspects of Divinity in the Tree of Life.

Kemetic Karest mas Celebration & Education

Ka Ab Ba corresponds with the Divine Trinity of Auset, Heru and Ausar

© Copyright Dr Nteri Nelson

- You can see here in the Tree of Life: The 3 Aspects of Divinity which are:
  - Auset/Ka/Mother/Spirit/Matter
  - Heru/Ab/Sun/Son/Daughter/Soul
  - Ausar Ba/Father/Soul/Spirit

Kemetic Karest mas Celebration & Education

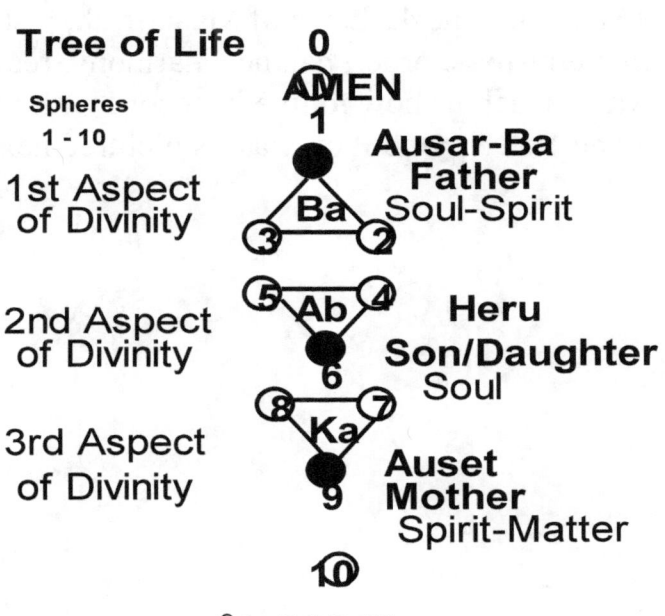

Symbol reclaimed and incorporated is:
- Maat and the 42 Laws of Maat, truth, justice, righteousness, order, balance, harmony, reciprocity, which teach us how to live in accord with nature.
- The Neter, symbol of Maat is pictured next.

Kemetic Karest mas Celebration & Education

42 Laws of Maat

Symbol reclaimed and incorporated is:
- The 42 Laws of Maat, is pictured next.
- Out of our corpus of Law, The Ten Commandments would later be derived, as seen in this next picture.
- In our Karest mas Celebration & Education let us move beyond The Ten Commandments, a reduced version, to re incorporate the 42 Laws of Maat.

Kemetic Karest mas Celebration & Education

THE 42 DECLARATIONS OF INNOCENSE The Admonitions of Maat

1. I HAVE NOT DONE INIQUITY.	22. I HAVE NOT POLLUTED MYSELF.
2. I HAVE NOT ACTED WITH VIOLENCE (TO ANYONE OR ANYTHING).	23. I HAVE NOT CAUSED TERROR.
3. I HAVE NOT ROBBED WITH VIOLENCE.	24. I HAVE NOT SPOKEN EVIL.
4. I HAVE DONE NO MURDER, I HAVE DONE NO HARM.	25. I HAVE NOT BURNED WITH RAGE.
5. I HAVE NOT DEFRAUDED TEMPLE OFFERINGS.	26. I HAVE NOT STOPPED MY EARS AGAINST THE WORDS OF RIGHT AND TRUTH (MAAT).
6. I HAVE NOT DIMINISHED OBLIGATIONS.	27. I HAVE NOT WORKED GRIEF.
7. I HAVE NOT PLUNDERED THE NETCHER.	28. I HAVE NOT ACTED WITH INSOLENCE.
8. I HAVE NOT SPOKEN LIES.	29. I HAVE NOT STIRRED UP STRIFE.
9. I HAVE NOT SNATCHED AWAY FOOD.	30. I HAVE NOT JUDGED HASTILY.
10. I HAVE NOT CAUSED PAIN.	31. I HAVE NOT BEEN AN EAVESDROPPER OR PRIED INTO MATTERS TO MAKE MISCHIEF.
11. I HAVE NOT ABUSED MY SEXUALITY.	32. I HAVE NOT MULTIPLIED MY WORDS EXCEEDINGLY.
12. I HAVE NOT CAUSED THE SHEDDING OF TEARS.	33. I HAVE NOT DONE HARM NOR ILL.
13. I HAVE NOT DEALT DECEITFULLY.	34. I HAVE NOT DISHONORED THE ANCESTORS.
14. I HAVE NOT TRANSGRESSED OR ANGERED GOD.	35. I HAVE NOT FOULED OR WASTED THE WATER.
15. I HAVE NOT ACTED GUILEFULLY.	36. I HAVE NOT SPOKEN SCORNFULLY.
16. I HAVE NOT LAID WASTE THE PLOUGHED LAND.	37. I HAVE NOT CURSED THE NETCHER.
17. I HAVE NOT BORN FALSE WITNESS.	38. I HAVE NOT POLLUTED THE EARTH.
18. I HAVE NOT SET MY LIPS IN MOTION (AGAINST ANYONE).	39. I HAVE NOT DEFRAUDED THE OFFERINGS OF THE NETERU.
19. I HAVE NOT BEEN ANGRY AND WRATHFUL EXCEPT FOR A JUST CAUSE.	40. I HAVE NOT PLUNDERED THE OFFERINGS OF THE BLESSED DEAD.
20. I HAVE NOT COMMITTED ADULTERY (not taken the wife of any man, the husband of any wife).	41. I HAVE NOT MISTREATED CHILDREN.
21. I HAVE NOT LUSTED NOR COMMITED FORNICATION.	42. I HAVE NOT MISTREATED ANIMALS.

Symbol reclaimed and incorporated is:
- The Weighing of the Heart in the Judgment Scene of the Hall of Amenta, Hall of Double Truth. This is key to our Karest mas Celebration.
- We see in the next picture that the heart (placed on the left hand side pan of the scale) is weighed against the lightness of the Feather of Maat (on the right hand side pan of the scale).
- As we prepare to come before the Neb, Lord of the World Ausar, we want our heart to be as light as the feather of Maat.
- This means that as Heru, the purificatory fires of our heart have done the work of transmuting all the heavy matters of life that we have faced like anger, jealousy, cruelty, self pity, bitterness, grief and so on, that make the heart heavy like lead, and to go 'clunk' against the lightness of the feather, on the scale of Maat.
- We have transmuted all the coarseness and pains of existence in our lives into a healing balm (not to be confused with bomb) a Spiritual substance, that is luminous, light filled and can be used to salve, soothe and heal the world and its inhabitants.
- Produced in the purificatory, fiery chambers of our own hearts, this radiatory substance contrib.- utes to the 'glow', light, and 'presence', of those who have done this work within themselves and which now radiates out to others.

Kemetic Karest mas Celebration & Education

The Weighing of The Heart

The Judgment Scene Hall of Amenta
Psychostasia:
The Judgment of the Heart of Ani
From the Funerary papyrus of Ani

- The 'heavy metal' of this world transmuted into pure gold by the heart is the Spiritual 'bling', prize, presents and treasure.
- Led by the Heru within us, we have become light-filled, and a 'presence' that can now stand before the 'Awesome Presence', Ausar, who is within the Divine Shrine (at the right in the next picture). Before Ausar, who is Neb, Lord of the World we are found innocent and Maa Kheru or True of Voice.
- Not to be confused with presents or packages at Christmas, brought by Santa Clause as we see how this concept has been distorted.

Kemetic Karest mas Celebration & Education

Symbol reclaimed and incorporated is:
- Let us reclaim the symbol Ausar, who is slain by his jealous brother Set and the evergreen tree of beautiful scent, called the Tamarisk Tree, which grew around the sarcophagus/coffin in which Ausar rested, once it had drifted along the Nile to Byblos.

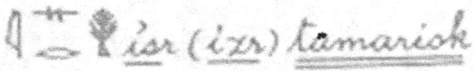

- This is very significant in our re acquisition of a Kemetic Karest mas Celebration.
- The Tree of Life is a divine template for Building The Lighted Temple, that we indwell.
- By reconnecting with our Kemetic Science we see the way to Build our own 'monumental' temple symbolized by the Karest mas Tree, in the next pictures and pages that follow .

In this next picture here we have the Tamarisk tree which surrounds Ausar.

Kemetic Karest mas Celebration & Education

© Melnik shutterstock

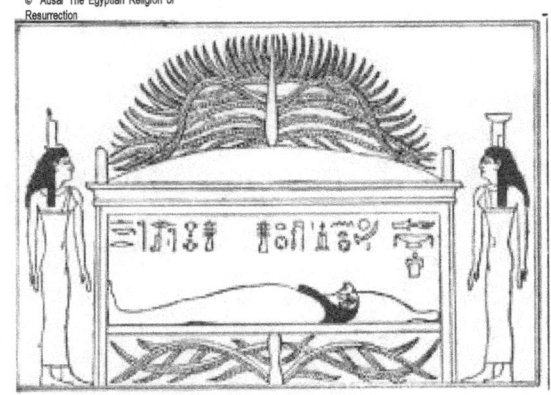

© Ausar The Egyptian Religion of Resurrection

© Copyright Dr Nteri Nelson

- Long ago in my book, *Ka Ab Ba Building The Lighted Temple,* I dispel the word Tamarisk to reveal the word Christmas, almost spelled backwards, as seen in this next picture.
- As we ungarble our symbols, we understand rightly.

Kemetic Karest mas Celebration & Education

Let's dispell the word tamarisk:

- **#10. Oracle Metaphysical Dis-Spelling Key:** Letter replacement. Here we have replaced the 'k' which had been substituted by the letter 'c.'
- **Derived Word List:**
- <u>Kristmas, C(h)ristmas</u> – as in Christmas Tree.

T
k
    a
s
    m
i
    a
r

© Copyright Dr Nteri Nelson

Symbol reclaimed and incorporated is:
- The 7 Planes of Consciousness or 7 Soul Bodies, symbolized by the Tree and given to us by our ancient texts, is pictured next.
- By detailing these, which they name Ba, Khu, Sekhem, Ab, Sahu, Ka/Khaibit and Khat, our ancestors have given us the blueprint for constructing our Temple and a world.

Kemetic Karest mas Celebration & Education

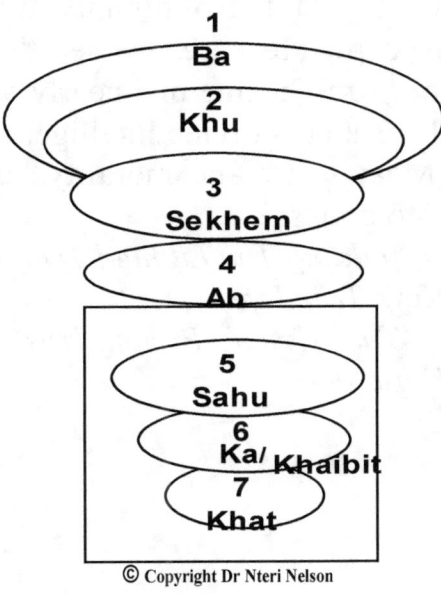

Symbol reclaimed and incorporated is:
- The Paut Neteru, the company of the Gods who imbrue us with qualities of divinity in our journey.
- In this next picture here, we see the Tree of Life laid out in a straight line or linearly and we see the Neteru, like Tehuti - divine intelligence, Herukhuti - strength, Maat - law and morality, and so on. For more refer to books:

◦ *Ka Ab Ba Building The Lighted Temple/Metaphysical Keys Tree Life;*

◦ *KaAbBa: The Great Pyramid is The Tree of Life:MerKaBa.*

Kemetic Karest mas Celebration & Education

MerKaBa Tree Of Life

AMEN 0

W/Ausar 1

Seker 3

Tehuti 2

Herukhuti 5

Ma'at 4

Heru 6

Sebek 8

Het Heru 7

Auset 9

Khnemu

Nit

© Dr Terri Nelson

™

Geb 10

Symbol reclaimed and incorporated is:
- The MerKaBa Energy Body of Light
- The MerKaBa is seen in this next picture at right, as we move deeper in our monument construction.
- The MerKaBa, is pictured as the double Pyramid, one above and one below, with the Square in between.
- The Tree of Life is the Great Pyramid MerKaBa.
- How does the Tree of Life become the MerKaBa?
- We are not crucified upon the Tree, rather in our journey, we are the Tree of Life, that now bends over backwards upon itself, like in the Nut posture, like the Sankofa symbol, like the serpent swallowing its tail (also pictured here).

Kemetic Karest mas Celebration & Education

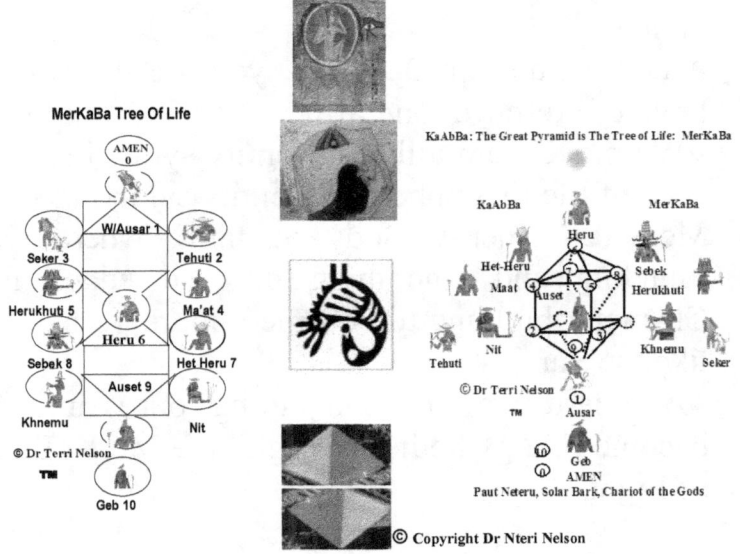

- As Heru, we are bending over backwards, we are 'knitting' ourselves back together again, we are uniting the seeming dualities of Ka and Ba, Spirit and Matter, Mother and Father, Ausar and Auset, Masculine and Feminine, the North and South Poles within your Constitution which is both human and divine.
- As the Sun-Son/Daughter, you are the Ka-rest, a Divine 'Presence' on Earth.
- We move from a linear identity symbolized by the Tree of life to a Spherical identity symbolized by the MerKaBa Energy Body of light, where we are rounding and smoothing out the edges in our Character building to become a more perfect sphere like the Sun.
- As Heru we are completing our Circuitry to become Energy bodies of Light, the MerKaBa Body of Light.

Kemetic Karest mas Celebration & Education

The KaAbBa:MerKaBa
Luminous Energy Body of Light

KaAbBa: The Great Pyramid is The Tree of Life: MerKaBa

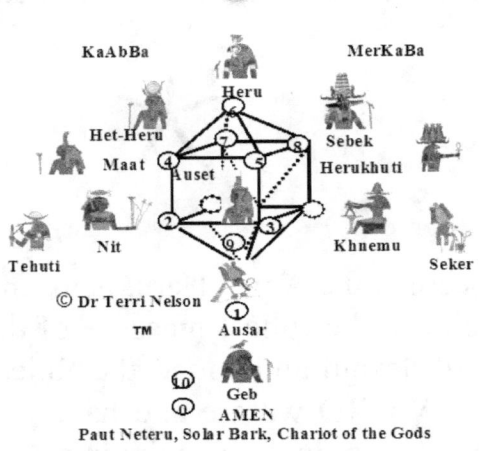

© Dr Terri Nelson
™

Paut Neteru, Solar Bark, Chariot of the Gods

© Copyright Dr Nteri Nelson

- It is in the bringing together of Ba and Ka that Ab becomes the spark within you. It is how you Build The Lighted Temple. At first, it is a faint glimmer of light. Like any spark, flicker or flame it must be kept guarded until it grows into a brilliantly, raging glow of fiery luminous Light.

- This is called the *Amsu Heru* by the Kemetians. and is symbolized by the 5 pointed Star, pictured here:

- To become the Amsu Heru, is to 'measure up' and achieve the fullest measure of the divinely intended design and sound the fullest measure of THE WORD we are and have always been from the beginningless beginning.
- As we complete our Circuitry, we become Luminous Spheres of light. We have Spherical Consciousness, with 1st Eye Activation, the ability to see unity, part, and relationship between.

Kemetic Karest mas Celebration & Education

- The Tree of life is the Great Pyramid, The MerKaBa.
- The MerKaBa Energy Body of Light is our Vehicle of:
  - 1st Eye Spherical Consciousness
  - Rebirth
  - Transformation
  - Resurrection
  - Ascension
  - Transport
  - Empowerment
  - Enlightenment
  - Initiation
  - Service

To learn more about the Amsu Heru, Sahu, and The MerKaBa, see:
◦ *Ka Ab Ba BuildingThe Lighted Temple/ Metaphysical Keys Tree Life and*
◦ *KaAbBa: The Great Pyramid is The Tree of Life: MerKaBa.*

Symbol reclaimed and incorporated is:

- In the bending back of the Tree of Life, the radiant heart of Heru, the Sun, rises to the apex of the Great Pyramid Giza, called the Mer Akhutu, as indicated by the arrow. This rising is the Resurrection of the Son/Daughter, which we call Heru the Karest, the bright Star of re-ascension.
- This is the crowning and seating of Heru upon his/her throne as heir to the Kingdom. As the Sun-Son/Daughter, you are the Ka-rest, a Divine 'Presence' on Earth. Again, this is not to be distorted as the material 'presents' or packages, at Christmas time, brought by so called, Santa Claus.

Kemetic Karest mas Celebration & Education

In the bending back of the Tree of Life
the radiant Heart of Heru, the Sun,
rises to the apex of the Great Pyramid Giza,

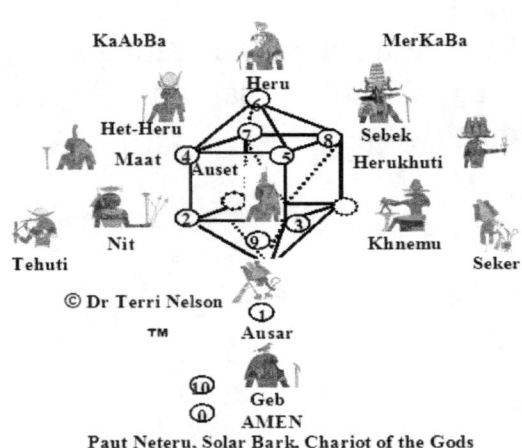

KaAbBa: The Great Pyramid is The Tree of Life: MerKaBa

Paut Neteru, Solar Bark, Chariot of the Gods

© Copyright Dr Nteri Nelson

Symbol reclaimed and incorporated is:
- As we knit ourselves back together again we undergo the Uniting of the North and South, within our own Spiritual Anatomy.
- We then reclaim the symbol of the Red and White Crown worn by Nesut Bity Narmer, who was King, ruler of Kemet around 5660 B.C.E.
- He united the North and the South of Kemet and was the first man recorded wearing the crown of unification.
- As Heru we undergo the seating as King upon our throne, as heir of Ausar and Auset, and to the Kingdom.

Kemetic Karest mas Celebration & Education

The Crowning and Seating of the King Heru upon his/her Throne, as heir of Ausar and Auset

- As Heru, you have united the seeming duality of Ka Ba, Mother Father, Ausar Auset, Matter Spirit, North South Poles within your Constitution which is both human and divine. This is the crowning and seating of Heru upon his/her throne as heir to the Kingdom. As the Sun-Son/Daughter, you are Divine 'Presence' on Earth. Not to be distorted as the material 'presents' at Christmas time at the so called birth of the son.

© Copyright Dr Nteri Nelson

- But the Kemetic White and Red crown of Kemet becomes distorted into the Santa Claus Hat of Christmas.
- We see here Pope Benedict XVI appearing at the Vatican wearing a Santa-style hat, known as a camauro.

Kemetic Karest mas Celebration & Education

The Kemetic White and Red crown of Kemet becomes distorted into the Santa Claus Hat

Pope Benedict XVI looked like he was getting into the festive spirit when he appeared at the Vatican wearing a Santa-style hat. The Pope appeared in St Peter's Square wearing a red cloak and a red velvet hat lined with white fur. Officials said the hat, known as a camauro, has been part of the papal wardrobe since the 12th century. It has not been worn in public since the death of John XXIII in 1963 reports BBC online.

© Copyright Dr Nteri Nelson

Symbol reclaimed and incorporated is:
- The Crook of Ausar would become the Candy Cane Of Christmas.
- The Crook is the symbol of how we carry our load and are aided to walk the narrow middle path of initiation.

Kemetic Karest mas Celebration & Education

Crook to Candy Cane

- It is no coincidence that we are attracted to Christmas and Christianity because it is derived out of Afrikan Divinity and Wisdom. In my work I have been relentless in dispelling the symbols that get us back to the root source and truth before it was co-opted.

Symbol reclaimed and incorporated is:
- The Djed/Tet Pillar, Symbol of Stability, the Backbone of Ausar.
- The Raising up of The Djed/Tet Pillar Causing it *to stand* was a celebration in Kemet, and this is key to our Karest mas Celebration & Education today.

Kemetic Karest mas Celebration & Education

A scene on the west wall of the Ausar Hall at Abtu/Abydos shows the raising of the *Djed* pillar

Symbol reclaimed and incorporated is:
- The Tamarisk, Erika, Evergreen, Sycamore, Acacia, Pine and Christmas Tree – all correspond with the Djed pillar.
- See the correspondence here on the next page between the Djed Pillar and the Tamarisk Tree *which I write more about in my books.*
- Now 'Raised' and caused to stand, The Tamarisk Tree is then adorned by the light of the Neteru spheres whose, divine energies, we call upon.
- We adorn the Tamarisk Tree with the Spheres of Neteru.

1

Kemetic Karest mas Celebration & Education

Djed/Tet
Pillar of Ausar
Symbol of Stability

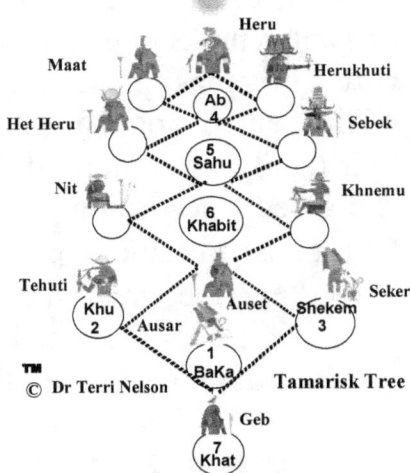

7 Soul Bodies of Kemetic Psychology & Spirituality

© Copyright Dr Nteri Nelson

Symbol reclaimed and incorporated is:
- The Sacred Boat on its Sledge
- Pictured at left is the Ark of the God Seker on its Sledge. The name given to the Seker Boat is "Hennu."
- When we dis-pell this symbol we see that the Sledge would later become the 'Sleigh' of Christmas. Notice the antlers in both pictures.
- The Sledge on the left bears the Divine 'Presence' of Deity, the Sleigh on the right bears Santa Claus with Christmas 'presents', or packages.
- This Sacred Boat has profound meaning in Afrikan Spirituality as glimpsed in the following passage expressed accordingly in, The Gods of the Egyptians: Volume 1, p. 505.*

> "On the great day of the festival of Seker which was celebrated in many places throughout Kemet, the ceremony of placing the Seker boat upon its sledge was performed at sunrise... under the direction of the high priest of Menefer...this official was expected to lift the Seker Boat upon its sledge, and to march at the head of the process...which drew the loaded sledge round the sanctuary. By this action

---

* Budge.

Kemetic Karest mas Celebration & Education

the revolution of the sun and other celestial bodies was symbolized..."

Sledge and Sleigh

Pictured at left is the Ark of the God Seker on its Sledge. The name given to the Seker Boat is "Hennu." When we dis-pell this symbol we see its lineage in what would later become the 'Sleigh'. Notice the antlers in both pictures. The Sledge on the left bears the Divine 'Presence' of Deity, the Sleigh on the right bears Santa Claus with Christmas 'Presents'.

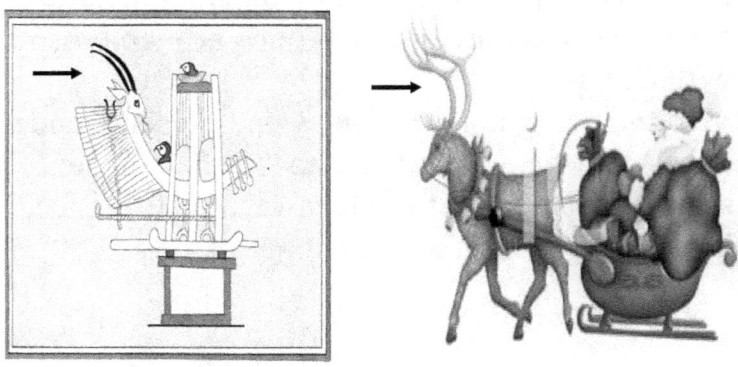

© Copyright Dr Nteri Nelson

Symbol reclaimed and incorporated (continued) is:
- That we may be the 'presence' that comes before the awesome 'Presence' of the Neb, Lord of the World, Ausar.
- How may we regain understanding, application and practice of ancient Afrikan wisdom in modern daily living that we overcome the materialistic consciousness now gripping our Earth and associated with Christmas.
- Do we want more packages and presents under the Xmas tree or do we want to be the 'Presence" we seek as we come before the awesome Presence, Neb, Lord of the World, Ausar?

Kemetic Karest mas Celebration & Education

● The Shemsu Heru

Those 'in the following' of Heru are called the Shemsu Heru. They are guided by the Heru/the Karest, that lives within them. It is the Heru that

lives within us, pictured here as the crowned Falcon headed Neter, who is leading Ani (who is us) who chooses to follow.
- Ani following and being led by Heru/who is 'within', and who is holding his hand, would later be translated biblically by Christianity as:

"I am the way and the truth and the life. No one comes to the Father except through me." John 14:6

Therefore, the Shemsu Heru are those who seek:
- To align their personal will with Divine Will, the Will of the Neb/Lord of the World, Ausar.
- To live in accord with the Laws of Maat.
- To be in Good Stewardship of the Earth and work for the uplift of the Kingdoms in nature, Mineral, Vegetable, Animal, Human, Spiritual.
- To sound the full vibrational sound of the One True Self as Ausar, which is to be found Maa Kheru, true of voice in how one lives and conducts their life.
- To be able to bear the vibration of coming within in the Presence, with a 'bow' before the Neb Lord of the World, Ausar.
- No longer to be confused with the Christmas presents 'nicely wrapped' with a 'bow' on top.
- We are the living, resurrected Karest, the Presence that comes before the Awesome Presence, Ausar, Neb, Lord of the World, and knows eternal life.
- Thus, My Father/Mother and I are one.

Kemetic Karest mas Celebration & Education

Chapter 3
▲ Steps To Preview & Actual Participation
∘In performing the Kemetic Karest mas Celebration let us move through the following:
▲ **Step 1** for **Preview**
∘Four directions, North, East, South and West/floor and room plan
∘See page 73 for **Actual Participation**.
▲ **Step 2** for **Preview**
∘Facing East (All)
∘Pour Libation to the Ancestors.
∘**Recitation from the Prt em Hru**
∘See page 74-76 for **Actual Participation**.
▲ **Step 3** for **Preview**
∘Facing West (All)
∘**Recitation from the Prt em Hru of the 42 Laws Maat/Declarations of Innocence**
∘Stand before the Scales of Maat where the feather of Maat has already been placed in the left hand pan of the scale. Imagine your own heart placed in the right hand pan and laying in balance with the feather of Maat. Recitation of the 42 Laws Maat, read each one out loud. (These are Admonitions of Innocence; that you have been in Good Stewardship of the Kingdoms in nature, mineral, vegetable, animal, human, spiritual.
∘See pages 76-77 for **Actual Participation**.
▲ **Step 4 a,b,c** for **Preview**

∘Facing South (All)
∘Lowering/Raising up Djed Pillar as symbolized by the Tamarisk tree/Pillar of Stability, Backbone of Ausar upon which the Sun rises.
∘**Recitation from the Prt em Hru**
∘See pages 78-84 for **Actual Participation**.
▲ **Step 5a,b,** for **Preview**
∘Adorn the Evergreen Tamarisk Tree with a sphere for each Neteru/Lighting the Tree.
∘See pages 84-86 for **Actual Participation**
▲ **Step 5c** for **Preview**
∘Recite the Qualities of each Neteru as each is being adorned upon the Tamarisk Tree.
∘See pages 88-99 for **Actual Participation**.
Step 5d for **Preview**
∘Djed/Tamarisk completely adorned
∘See pages 100-101 for **Actual Participation**.
▲ **Step 6** for **Preview**
∘Facing North. (All)
∘Recite the Hymn To Heru.
∘See pages 102-103 for **Actual Participation**.
▲ **Step 7a,b,c** for **Preview**
∘Facing East. (All)
∘Before alter and Shrine of Ausar, each family member come forth and says:
∘a. Which Quality of the Neteru, use <u>Key Word(s)</u> here, each one easily expresses, or is working to better express or cultivate more of
and/or

Kemetic Karest mas Celebration & Education

∘b. Which Law of Maat each one is working with in order to:
∘To have greater presence, Ausarian like Presence, standing before the Neb Lord of the World. To be of greater benefit to planet Earth and the Universe(s).'

∘See pages 104-107 for **Actual Participation**.
▲ **Step 8** for **Preview**
∘Circling around (Circumambulating) the room 7 times, one for each Plane of Consciousness, with the Djed/Tamarisk Evergreen Tree in the center, Sing Re-ascension into Sacredness.
∘See pages 108-110 for **Actual Participation**.
▲ **Step 9** for **Preview**
∘Feast with family and community upon your favorite nutritional foods.
∘Feast Spiritually on Sacred Symbols Revealed.
∘See pages 111-117 for **Actual Participation**.

▲ **Steps To Complete in ADVANCE**
COMPLETE ALL OF THESE STEPS BEFORE THE START OF YOUR KEMETIC KAREST MAS CELEBRATION
Step 10a
∘**What you will want to have on hand for your Celebration. See page 118 for list.**
Step 10b
∘Purchase and attach a stand to the base of the Tamarisk/Evergreen Tree. You and your family may

enjoy the beautiful scent of this real Tree, knowing more that it is the Djed Pillar, backbone of Ausar.

Step 10c

◦You may use seasonal white lights on the Djed Pillar/Tamarisk Tree, (optional). If so, adorn the Djed Pillar/Tamarisk Tree with strings of white lights.

Step 10d

◦Stand Tree in a corner of the room, preferably against a wall and drape with a white cloth, until the appointed time.

Step 10e

◦Place the name and image of each Neteru on a sphere or bulb, to adorn the Tree at the appointed time in the Celebration.

Step 10f

◦Preparing for the 'Lowering' and 'Raising' the Djed Pillar/Tamarisk Tree.

Step 10g

◦Choose one Community Mature male and one Community Mature female designated to 'lower' the Tree, into place, at the appointed time in the Celebration.

Step 10h

◦Choose one Young Adult male and one Young female designated to be 'raisers' or lifters of the Tree, at the appointed time in the Celebration.

Step 10i

Kemetic Karest mas Celebration & Education

∘Place a scale on a table in the West direction of the room. Place a feather of Maat on the right hand pan of the scale.

Step 10j Choose an Elder from your community to do/pour the Libation using a practice he/she is already familiar with/or use example on page 77.

Step 10K

∘Now that you have gathered your friends, family and community together you are ready to begin.

•Step 1
Four directions, North, East, South and West/floor and room plan.

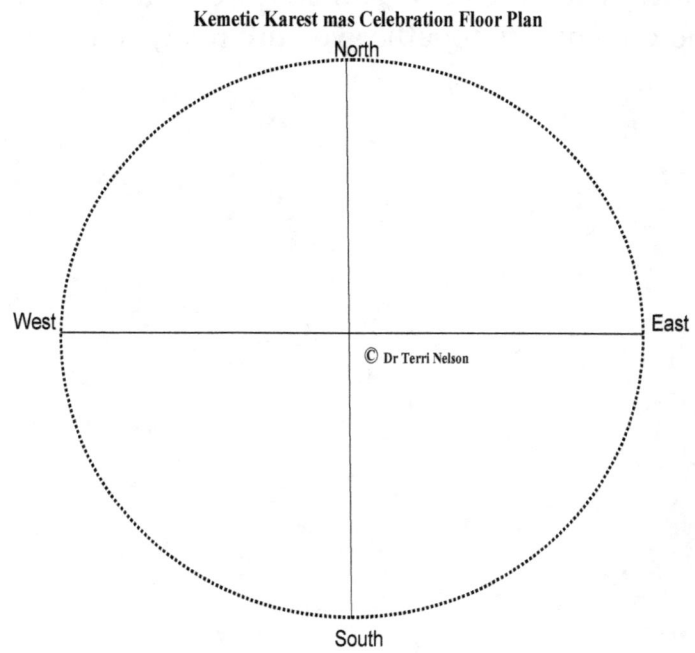

Kemetic Karest mas Celebration & Education

●Step 2
Facing East - all participants face in this direction. Pour Libation and give honor to the ancestors.

Libation
◦In praise and appreciation for the in gathering of our family, friends and community
•We pour libation and call upon:
◦AMEN, Infinite Eternal All in All, Neter Neteru, Fount of All Possibility.
◦Father/Mother Creator, Most High, Neb Lord of the World in Whom we live and move and have our being, Divined as AusarAuset, whose livinging-ness is expressed through us as Heru, the Karest within us.
◦We pour libation and call upon:
◦The Paut Neteru, the company of the Gods, guiding us into sacred space, imbruing us with all Divine Qualities, teaching us to live as Neteru Gods/Goddesses.
◦We pour libation and call upon:
◦The Names of our Ancestors who have gone before and call our blood relatives (ex., my great grandfather (name)...) etc.
◦We pour libation and call upon:
◦The Names of our Ancestors who have been our Heros/Sheros, who have made sacrifice in uplifting us in our struggle (ex., King Narmer, Frederick

Douglass, Queen Tiye, Rosa Parks, George James) etc.

◦We pour libation and call upon:
Those who have remained steady in the Light and Those with heavy laden and hard won footsteps who have trodden their way back into the Light and establish greater *Presence*, Ausarian Presence on planet Earth and the Universe(s), to be of greater benefit. In all praise and appreciation we give thanks that you hear our prayers.

Recitation from the Prt em Hru
◦*Chapter 26   Chapter of Giving a Heart Unto Heru _____ in the Underworld.*
(say your name here, ex. Heru Jamal)
Prt em Hru   p. 308 (Egyptian Book Of The Dead, E. A. Wallace Budge).
At the Eastern Alter:
Group Says:

"May my heart be with me in the "House of Hearts. May my heart be with me, and may it rest in me, or I "shall not eat of the cakes of Ausar on the eastern side of the Lake of Flowers, neither shall I have a boat wherein to go down the Nile, and another wherein to go up, nor shall I go forward in the boat with you. May my mouth be given to me that I may speak with it, and my two feet to walk with, and my two hands and arms to overthrow my foe. May the doors of heaven be opened unto me; may Geb/Seb,

Kemetic Karest mas Celebration & Education

the Prince of the gods, open wide his two jaws unto me; may he open my two eyes which are bound together; and may Anubis make my legs firm that I may stand upon them. May the goddess Sekhet make me to rise so that I may ascend unto heaven, and there may that be done which I command in the House of the Ka of Ptah. I know my heart, I have gotten the mastery over my heart, I have gotten the mastery over my two hands and arms, I have gotten the mastery over my feet, and I have gained the power to do whatsoever my Ka pleases. My soul shall not be shut off from my body at the gates of the underworld; but I shall enter in peace, and I shall come forth in peace."

Step 3
◦Facing West - all participants face in this direction, standing before the Scales.
◦**Recitation of the 42 Laws Maat, on next page.**
◦Each member reads out loud one by one, until all 42 Laws have been recited.

The Weighing of The Heart
The Judgment Scene Hall of Amenta
Psychostasia:
The Judgment of the Heart of Ani
From the Funerary papyrus of Ani

THE 42 DECLARATIONS OF INNOCENSE The Admonitions of Maat

1. I HAVE NOT DONE INIQUITY.	22. I HAVE NOT POLLUTED MYSELF.
2. I HAVE NOT ACTED WITH VIOLENCE (TO ANYONE OR ANYTHING).	23. I HAVE NOT CAUSED TERROR.
3. I HAVE NOT ROBBED WITH VIOLENCE.	24. I HAVE NOT SPOKEN EVIL.
4. I HAVE DONE NO MURDER, I HAVE DONE NO HARM.	25. I HAVE NOT BURNED WITH RAGE.
5. I HAVE NOT DEFRAUDED TEMPLE OFFERINGS.	26. I HAVE NOT STOPPED MY EARS AGAINST THE WORDS OF RIGHT AND TRUTH (MAAT).
6. I HAVE NOT DIMINISHED OBLIGATIONS.	27. I HAVE NOT WORKED GRIEF.
7. I HAVE NOT PLUNDERED THE NETCHER.	28. I HAVE NOT ACTED WITH INSOLENCE.
8. I HAVE NOT SPOKEN LIES.	29. I HAVE NOT STIRRED UP STRIFE.
9. I HAVE NOT SNATCHED AWAY FOOD.	30. I HAVE NOT JUDGED HASTILY.
10. I HAVE NOT CAUSED PAIN.	31. I HAVE NOT BEEN AN EAVESDROPPER OR PRIED INTO MATTERS TO MAKE MISCHIEF.
11. I HAVE NOT ABUSED MY SEXUALITY.	32. I HAVE NOT MULTIPLIED MY WORDS EXCEEDINGLY.
12. I HAVE NOT CAUSED THE SHEDDING OF TEARS.	33. I HAVE NOT DONE HARM NOR ILL.
13. I HAVE NOT DEALT DECEITFULLY.	34. I HAVE NOT DISHONORED THE ANCESTORS.
14. I HAVE NOT TRANSGRESSED OR ANGERED GOD.	35. I HAVE NOT FOULED OR WASTED THE WATER.
15. I HAVE NOT ACTED GUILEFULLY.	36. I HAVE NOT SPOKEN SCORNFULLY.
16. I HAVE NOT LAID WASTE THE PLOUGHED LAND.	37. I HAVE NOT CURSED THE NETCHER.
17. I HAVE NOT BORN FALSE WITNESS.	38. I HAVE NOT POLLUTED THE EARTH.
18. I HAVE NOT SET MY LIPS IN MOTION (AGAINST ANYONE).	39. I HAVE NOT DEFRAUDED THE OFFERINGS OF THE NETERU.
19. I HAVE NOT BEEN ANGRY AND WRATHFUL EXCEPT FOR A JUST CAUSE.	40. I HAVE NOT PLUNDERED THE OFFERINGS OF THE BLESSED DEAD.
20. I HAVE NOT COMMITTED ADULTERY (not taken the wife of any man, the husband of any wife).	41. I HAVE NOT MISTREATED CHILDREN.
21. I HAVE NOT LUSTED NOR COMMITED FORNICATION.	42. I HAVE NOT MISTREATED ANIMALS.

Kemetic Karest mas Celebration & Education

- **Step 4a**
  ◦ When your community completes the recitation of the 42 Laws of Maat, then all turn
  ◦ Facing South - all participants face in this direction
  Lowering the Djed Pillar/Tamarisk Tree
  ◦ A designated Mature male comes forth on the right and a Mature female comes forth on the left, brings the Tamarisk Tree forward, then gently 'lowers' or lays the Tree down in position, centered on the floor, with the top/head of the Tree facing South as indicated in the diagram.
  ◦ See diagram next page.
  ◦ This action symbolizes the entrance into the Judgment Scene of the Hall of Amenta, Hall of Double Truth - entrance into the tomb and the womb of rebirth.

[Note: The pronouns in the **Recitations from the Prt em Hru** that follow have been personalized for the benefit of the participant(s). Also, ones own name may recited in place of the name Ani, and is to be inserted when reading: Heru _____,
Participant's name
The excerpts are exactly from the **Prt em Hru** text, with minor adjustments in order to de- anglicize the text and speak in the 1st voice as Heru/Karest].

'Lowering' The Djed Pillar/Tamarisk Tree

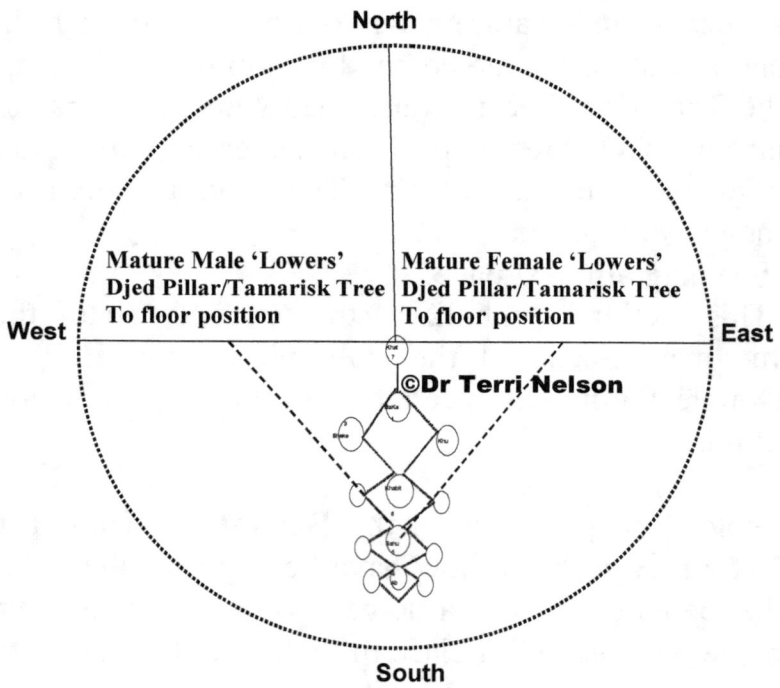

Turn book upside down to view this image, with Female standing on the left, Male on the Right. As the Tree is lowered into position of the tomb/ground/floor, the head/top of the Tree comes to rest here, facing South.

Kemetic Karest mas Celebration & Education

Chapters Of Coming Forth By Day. Prt em Hru p. 273. (Egyptian Book Of The Dead, E. A. Wallace Budge)
Group Says:
"O you who make perfected souls to enter into the Hall of Ausar, may you cause the perfected soul of Heru _____, to be victorious in the Hall of Double Truth, to enter with you into the house of Ausar. May I hear as you hear; may I see as you see; may I stand as you stand; may I sit as you sit!...May I enter in with a bold heart and may I come forth in peace from the house of Ausar. May I not be rejected, may I not be turned back, may I enter in as I please, may I come forth as I desire, and may I be victorious. May my bidding be done in the house of Ausar may I walk, and may I speak with you, and may I be a glorified soul along with you. I have not been found wanting there, and the Balance is rid of my trial."

◦Chapter 27
The Chapter of Not Letting The Heart Of A Man/Woman Be Taken Away From Him/Her In The Underworld. Prt em Hru p. 312. (Egyptian Book Of The Dead, E. A. Wallace Budge)
Group Says:
"... O you lords of eternity, you possessors of everlastingness, take you not away this heart of Heru _____. In your grasp, this heart of Heru. And cause you not evil words to spring up against

it. ... The heart of Heru _____ is pleasant unto the gods; I am victorious, I have gotten power over it... I have gotten power over my own limbs. My heart obeys me, I am the lord thereof... I am Heru _____, victorious in peace, and triumphant in the beautiful Amenta and on the mountain of eternity, bid you [my heart] be obedient unto me in the underworld."

◦Chapter 29A
The Chapter of The Heart Not Being Carried Away In The Underworld
 p. 313. Papyrus of Ani. Prt em Hru   (Egyptian Book Of The Dead, E. A. Wallace Budge)

Group Says:
"My heart is with me, and it shall never come to pass that it shall be carried away... I live in right and in truth, and I have my being therein. I am Heru, a pure heart within a pure body. I live by my word, and my heart does live. Let not my heart be taken away, let it not be wounded, and may no wounds or gashes be dealt upon me because it has been taken away from me. May I exist in the body of my father Geb/Seb, and in the body of my mother Nut. I have not done evil against the gods; I have not sinned with boasting."

Kemetic Karest mas Celebration & Education

○ Chapter 46
The Chapter of The Heart Not Perishing And Of Becoming Alive In The Underworld. p. 316, Papyrus of Ani. Prt em Hru (Egyptian Book Of The Dead, E. A. Wallace Budge)

Group Says

"Heru_____, Hail Children of Shu! Hail Children of Shu, children of the place of the dawn, who as the children of light have gained possession of his/her crown. May I rise up and may I fare forth like Ausar."

Step 4b
Raising of the Karest mas, Tamarisk, Isar, Ausar Tree/Djed Pillar
○ The Young Adult male Raiser comes forth and stands on the right side and the Young Adult female Raiser stands on the left side, of the Tree.
○ Using one rope that has been tied to the top part (neck) of Tree and evenly divided between the two raisers/lifters, both 'Raise' the Tree to a 'Standing' position at the same time.

Step 4c
○ Remove cord/rope.
○ See diagram next page.
○ It is the uniting of balanced male and female energy that cause birth and re-birth. The cord is a symbol of birth.

Raising The Djed/Tamarisk Tree

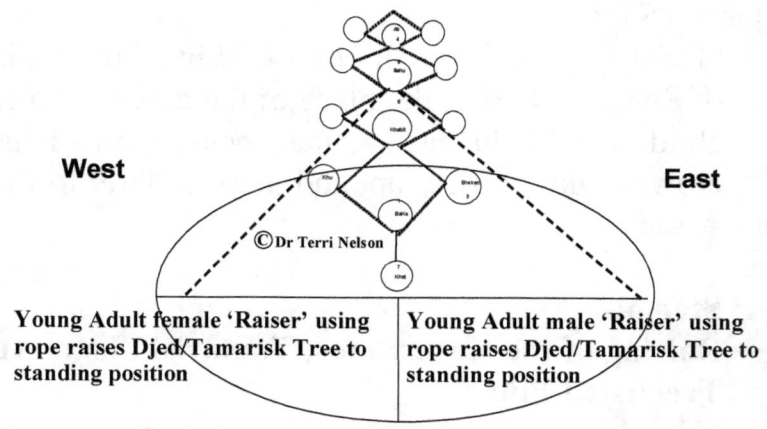

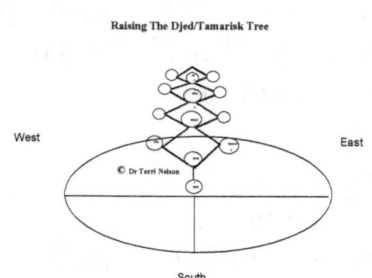

Kemetic Karest mas Celebration & Education

◦**Recitation from the Prt em Hru**
◦Chapter 9
The Chapter of Coming Forth By Day, Having Passed Through The Tomb
p. 321. Papyrus of Ani. Prt em Hru (Egyptian Book Of The Dead, E. A. Wallace Budge)
"Hail Soul, you mighty one of strength. Truly I am here, I have come, I behold you. I have passed through the underworld, I have seen my father Ausar, I have scattered the gloom of night. I am his beloved one. I have come; I behold my father Ausar. I have stabbed Set to the heart. I have done the things needed by my father Ausar. I have opened every way in heaven and upon earth. I am the son/daughter beloved of my father Ausar. I have become a ruler, I have become glorious, I am furnished with what I need. Hail, all you gods, and all you shining ones, make you a way for me, the son/daughter of Ausar, Heru – triumphant."

Step 5a
◦**Adorning of the Karest mas, Tamarisk Tree, Isar, Ausar Tree/Djed Pillar**
◦Adorning the Tree with Spheres of Neteru while
◦Reciting the Divine Qualities of each Sphere as it is being placed upon the Tree.
Step 5b

◦Order the adorning of the Neteru spheres according to picture as shown on the next page.
◦Sphere 1 Ausar and Auset are placed upon the Tree at the same time by a designated Young Adult male and Young Adult female from your family, friends, community.
◦Sphere 2 - 8 are placed upon the Tree by randomly designated Children, in an ascending order up the Tree, as indicated in the picture.
◦Sphere 9 Heru is placed at the top of the Tree, by a tall(er) female Youth, together with a male Youth who places the 5 Pointed Star, The Amsu Heru, Crowning Light upon the Tree.
◦Sphere10 Geb is placed last, at the bottom of the Tree, by a shorter youth, as symbolizing the manifesting of Light, Heaven on Earth.

Step 5c
◦At the same time community participants take a turn, coming forward and reading the qualities of each Neteru as it Sphere is being placed.
◦See qualities of Neteru pages 88-95.

Kemetic Karest mas Celebration & Education

Order of Adorning
Spheres of the Neteru
Lightening Flash of Re Ascension

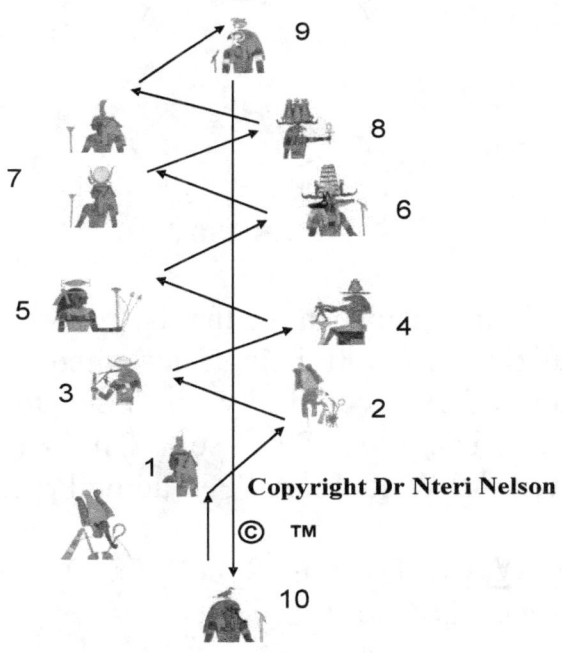

Copyright Dr Nteri Nelson
© ™

Bringing Heaven to Earth

Qualities of the Neteru
Color Art Work Drawing of each Neter
By Artist Ptah Seeker Ausaures

W/Ausar

The divine quality in me that is:
Realizing my full being, unlimited access to the Fount of All Possibility in order to achieve all things. The One True Self. The Drawer of All Power, All Wisdom, All Pervading Presence.

Key Word: The One True Self, Omnipresence/All Presence, Divine Will.

Kemetic Karest mas Celebration & Education

Auset

The divine quality in me that is:
• Persevering, ceaseless devotion in re-gathering the broken body of Ausar, desiring the luminous mirror-image reflection of the Divine Father upon the emotional, impregnable, imagistic waters of the Divine Mother. The remembrance of the Marriage between the Divine Neter, Father & Mother, Spirit & Matter. The womb, nurturing and birthing the One True Self which is me.

Key Word: Nurturing & Birthing the One True Self.

Tehuti

The divine quality in me that is:
Intuiting, Divine intelligence, ideation, Wisdom, Love. Underlying Unity, knowledge of whole, part and the perfect relationship between. Glimpsing the divinely intended architectural design and plan for manifestation, pure and perfect without distortion or flaw. Illuminating Light and Higher Mind. All knowing, omniscience.

Key Word: Omniscience/All knowing, Divine Wisdom & Love.

Kemetic Karest mas Celebration & Education

Seker

The divine quality in me that is:
• Drawing the vibrational circle that contains the greatest good; creating structure and setting limits within which full creative potential, power and intelligence is to be achieved. Circumscribing the field(s) of experience and allotting space and time in which Divine Purpose is to be made manifest. Authoritatively sounding the Hekau-word of power, demanding the full vibrational sounding and expression of the One True SELF in the, to-be manifested form(s), of my becoming. Powering the goal of the Archetypal Design in achieving my intended purpose in fullness through graduated 'Ring-Pass-Nots' of boundaried experiences.

Key Word: Omnipotence/All Power, Divine Intelligence.

Nit

The divine quality in me that is:
- Conceiving and bringing forth the new Sun-Son/Daughter god daily, which is me. Using tools of creation, knitting and weaving perfect light form(s), to which the earthy dust element of densification of Khnemu is added and both together are the fabric or garment of Neteru/God. Fashioning my 'finest robes', my best 'threads' spun with Supper Atomic sub-stance, tiniest particles of 'bubbly' Light, *so fine* that scientists are still trying to figure out how to 'see' and 'identify' the Spherical Luminous Body of Light that I am. Protecting and maintaining the Highest Light, so that no-thing that is unrepresentative of the Neteru/God is allowed to come into manifest-tation. Mother of mothers and Father of fathers.

<u>Key Word:</u> Precision Tools of Creating.

Kemetic Karest mas Celebration & Education

Khnemu

The divine quality in me that is:
•Conceiving and bringing forth the new Sun-Son/Daughter god daily, which is me. Using tools of creation, building, uniting, molding myself. Adding the earthy dust element to the perfect light form(s) of Nit, which both together are the fabric or garment of Neteru/God, I am fashioning my 'finest robes', my best 'threads' spun with super atomic sub-stance *so fine* that scientists are still trying to figure out how to 'see' and 'identify' the Spherical Luminous Body of Light that I am. Releasing or holding back the flood waters of the Nile, source of things which exist, creator of things which shall be. Father of fathers, and Mother of mothers

Key Word: Precision Tools of Creating

Het Heru

The divine quality in me that is:
• Glimpsing, through higher abstract mind and imagination Inner Archetypal Patterning of beauty. Aspiring towards, lovingly and magnetically attracting the higher ideal and greater wholeness. Mediating discordant energies and creating harmony (concordance) in relationships. Aspirating for The One True Self. Artistically and creatively engaging energy along the spinal column/Djed Pillar, to ascend through planes of consciousness.

Key Word: Art, Beauty, Greater Wholeness.

Kemetic Karest mas Celebration & Education

Sebek

The divine quality in me that is:
•Clothing Divine Ideation in thought-form(s), making it tangible in the concrete mind, applicable in the real world, where both cycles of draught and floods, abundance and poverty prevail. Critically thinking, accumulating knowledge, problem solving, planning, reasoning, analyzing data and particularizing, discerning, and examining parts. Grounding higher ideation and ideals into practical life solutions and communicating ideas.

Key Word: Thinking, Reasoning, Communicating.

Maat

The divine quality in me that is:
Upholding truth, justice, righteousness, order, balance, harmony, reciprocity, and Right Relationship in order to live in accord with Universal Laws of Nature. Honoring the Essential Self in All and the Web of interdependence between all created beings. Embracing philosophy of Wisdom that embraces all. Right working together with might (Love and Will).

Key Word: Justice, Right Relationship, Harmony.

Kemetic Karest mas Celebration & Education

Herukhuti

The divine quality in me that is:
•The right of asserting courageously the fullness of the One True Self while upholding the right of others to assert the same One True Self Identity - in fullness. Might and Right (Will and Love) working together. Triumphant warrior and defender of the Right.

Key Word: Assertion, Strength, Might & Right.

Heru

The divine quality in me that is:
•Making choices that bend personal will into alignment with Divine Will and is triumphant over Set. The Karest within me, the radiating heart of Intelligent, Loving, Will. Building in conscious accord and co-creative participation in the Divinely intended design, purpose and plan for my life. Growing soul conscience and consciousness. Fulfilling my life purpose.

Key Word: Karest, Divinely Aligned Will, Co-Creativ Sun – Son/Daughter.

Kemetic Karest mas Celebration & Education

Geb/Seb

The divine quality in me that is:
•Manifesting the living-ness of the Neteru/God indwelling within me. Spirit and Matter at work, visibly and tangibly expressing, Heaven on Earth. Through me, the divinely patterned world of beauty, peace (Hotep), harmony, abundance, are made manifest. Living Divinity walking on Earth. Building the Lighted Temple and a world in accord with the Laws of Maat.

Key Word: Manifesting Heaven on Earth. Building The Lighted Temple.

Step 5d
◦The Djed Pillar/Tamarisk Tree now fully adorned with Spheres of Neteru is pictured next.

Please Note:
◦In dispelling the words:
Adorn - to enhance the beauty, splendor or glory of, to add luster to.
Adore - to worship.
Adonai - Lord, spoken substitute for the ineffable name of God.
Ardor - intense heat or glow.

◦Meaning Derived is:
We are 'adorning' the Tree. We are not 'hanging' anything on the Tree. When we adorn the Neteru Spheres upon the Tree, we are recognizing the qualities of divinity that are within us and radiantly shining through us. Something or someone 'hangs' if it is separate and affixed to something higher than itself.

Kemetic Karest mas Celebration & Education

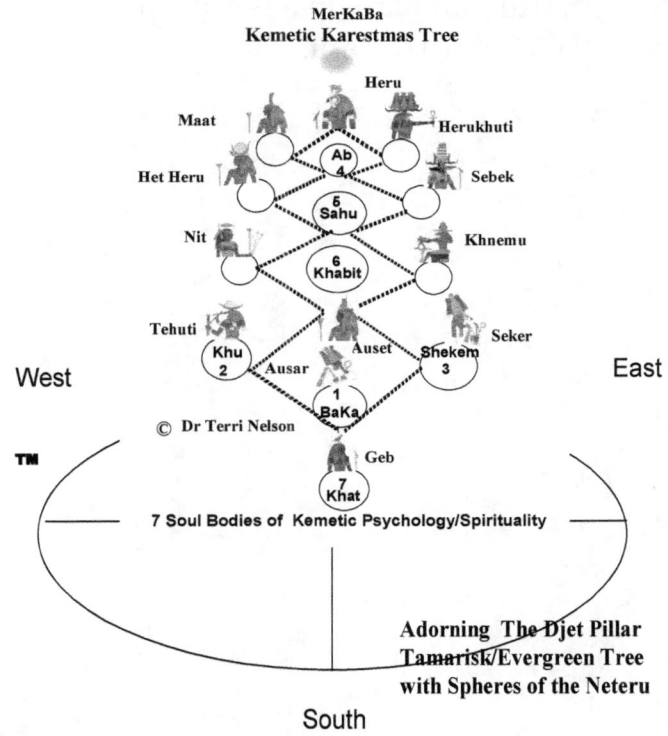

- **Step 6**
  ◦ Facing North - all participants face in this direction.
  ◦ Recite the Hymn To Heru.

Kemetic Karest mas Celebration & Education

A Hymn To Heru

From the Metu Neter text
"Heru is the savior who was brought to birth, as light in heaven and sustenance on earth. Heru in spirit, verily divine, who came to turn the water into wine. Heru who gave his life, and sowed the seed for men to make the bread of life indeed. Heru, the comforter, who did descend in human fashion as the heavenly friend. Heru, the word, the founder in youth, Heru, the fulfiller of the word made truth. Heru, the Lord and leader in the fight against the dark powers of the night. Heru, the sufferer with cross bowed down, who rose at Easter with his double crown. Heru the pioneer, who paved the way of resurrection to the eternal day Heru triumphant with battle done, Lord of two worlds, united and made one."*

---

* Budge. *Prt Em Hru.* (*Egyptian Book of The Dead*).

Step 7a
◦Facing East - all participants face in this direction.

Step 7b
a. Choose one Neter and Recite its *Key Word(s.)* the Positive Qualities you are expressing or working to better express.
See page 103.

Or/

b. Choose one Law of Maat you are expressing or working to better express.
See page 77.

Step 7c
◦Standing or kneeling (if you choose) before the alter and Shrine of Ausar, Neb, Lord of the World
◦Each community/family member comes forth and says:

Kemetic Karest mas Celebration & Education

'Ausar, Neb, Lord of the World.
I_____
  (name)
come as a presence to stand before and within your 'Awesome Presence'.

In order that I may have greater, Ausarian like Presence, I am working to express the
Qualities of/
  Or
Law of Maat/
_____,
  (choose a. and/or b, see next page).
to be of greater benefit to planet Earth and the Universe(s).'

Example: Quality of the Neteru
∘Ausar, Neb, Lord of the World.
∘ 'I__Heru Kingston Ra
come as a presence to stand before and within your 'Awesome Presence'.
∘I am working to express the Divine Qualities of Het Heru, Art, Beauty, Greater Wholeness.
∘In order that I may have greater, Ausarian like Presence and be of greater benefit to planet Earth and the Universe(s).'

Example: Law of Maat
∘Ausar, Neb, Lord of the World.
∘ 'I__Heru Kingston Ra
come as a presence to stand before and within your 'Awesome Presence'.
∘I am working on The Law of Maat, 'Not Snatching Away' Food.
∘I fulfill my family obligations of putting food on the table.
∘In order that I may have greater, Ausarian like Presence and be of greater benefit to planet Earth and the Universe(s).'

Kemetic Karest mas Celebration & Education

Neteru Divine Qualities: *Key Words*

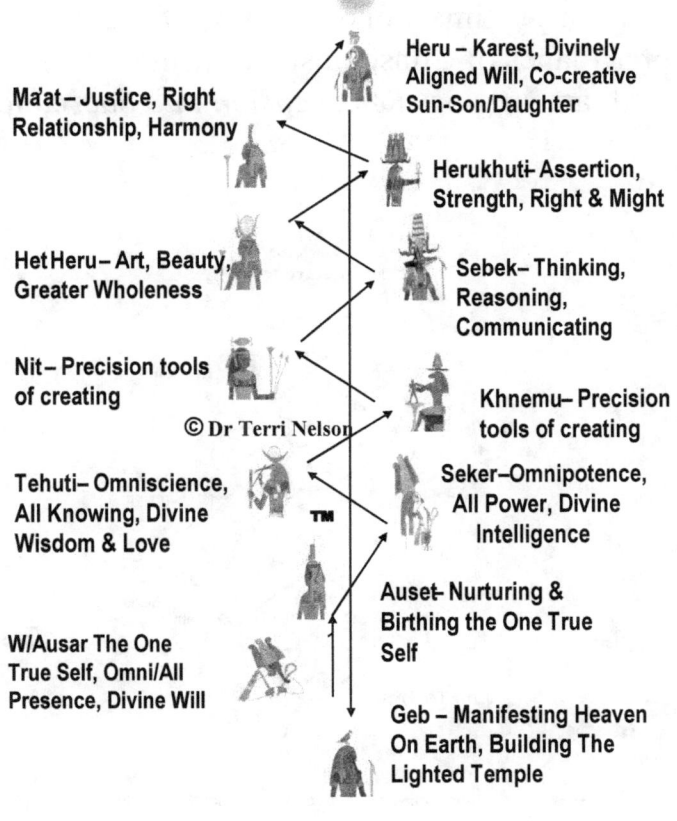

Heru – Karest, Divinely Aligned Will, Co-creative Sun-Son/Daughter

Ma'at – Justice, Right Relationship, Harmony

Herukhuti– Assertion, Strength, Right & Might

HetHeru – Art, Beauty, Greater Wholeness

Sebek – Thinking, Reasoning, Communicating

Nit – Precision tools of creating

© Dr Terri Nelson

Khnemu– Precision tools of creating

Tehuti– Omniscience, All Knowing, Divine Wisdom & Love

Seker–Omnipotence, All Power, Divine Intelligence

Auset– Nurturing & Birthing the One True Self

W/Ausar The One True Self, Omni/All Presence, Divine Will

Geb – Manifesting Heaven On Earth, Building The Lighted Temple

Step 8

◦ Circling around (circumambulating) Counter-Clockwise around the Tamarisk Tree (in the center of room) 7 times, one for each of the 7 Soul Bodies or 7 Planes of Consciousness, while

◦ All are singing, *Re ascension into Sacredness*.

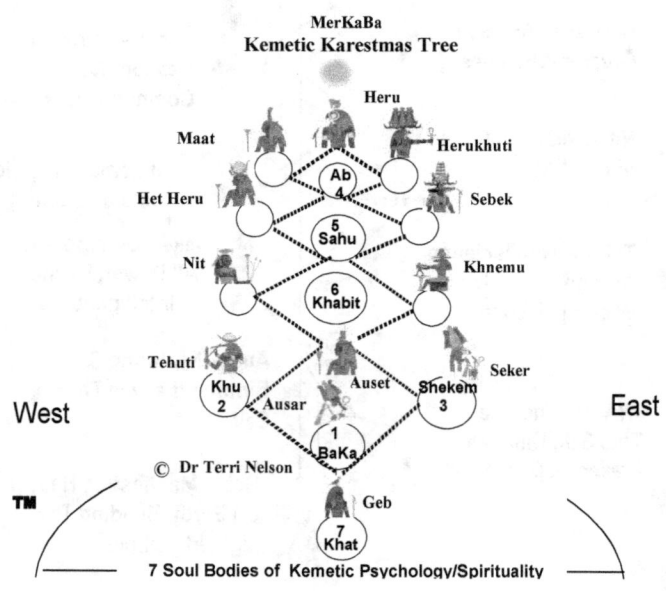

For more advanced study of the content refer to:
◦ *Ka Ab Ba BuildingThe Lighted Temple/ Metaphysical Keys Tree Life* and
◦ *KaAbBa: The Great Pyramid is The Tree of Life: MerKaBa*

Kemetic Karest mas Celebration & Education

Reascension Into Sacredness
   from the Elders
Communicated via
 Dr. Terri Nelson

Re-ascension into sacredness
All are gathering in

Re-ascension into sacredness
From the four winds

Our Elders are elated
By the dawning of this hour
They stand in witness to this day
Feel their great power
        (repeat 1st verse)

We emerge from the darkness
Eons long was night
We come now to serve and save
The rising Sun's in sight.
        (repeat 1st verse)

Reascension Into Sacredness

Dr. Terri Nelson

Kemetic Karest mas Celebration & Education

Step 9
∘Feast with family and community upon your favorite nutritional foods.

Most Sacred of Symbols Revealed

Symbol reclaimed and incorporated is:
- Let us reclaim the Symbol of Re-ascension Up the Tree of Life and Manifesting Heaven as a Light and Presence on Earth.
- As the action of Re-ascension Up The Djed/Tamarisk symbol is taking place it has correspondence with the symbol, Imiut, pictured in the Shrine of Ausar. This Symbol is pictured on next page alongside the Tamarisk Tree of Life.
- We are the Sacred Bull/Cow, who is making ascent up the Tree of Life through the 7 Het Heru Planes of Consciousness.
- We are wrapped within the cow skin, wrapping around this pole of ascent. As we ascend the pole or planes of consciousness we are 'rung' of all the fragrant scent, or essence, of our hard efforts at Character Building, as symbolized by the Lotus Flower which culminates on top of the Imiut.
- It is how we in our journey 'gut' wrenchingly, bending over backwards, turning ourselves upside down and inside out, 'ring' ourselves out, in order to indwell all the Planes of Consciousness and to be a greater light on the Earth, as Consciousness is awakened in us.

Kemetic Karest mas Celebration & Education

●Imiut - in Metu Neter (translates to "he who is in his wrappings")

Imiut

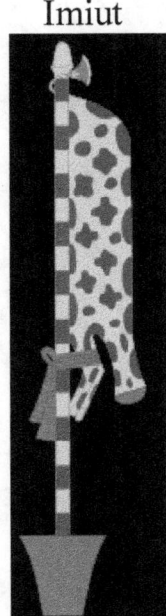

Order of Adorning Spheres of the Neteru Lightening Flash of Re Ascension

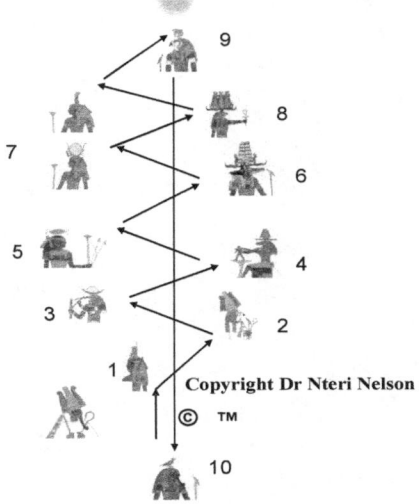

Copyright Dr Nteri Nelson © ™

Bringing Heaven to Earth

- To be in ones wrappings is to have knit oneself back together again.
- To wrap is to 'rap', to sound the full vibrational sound of the One True Self, which is us. To be in one's rappings is to be rapped as a Presence, a Presence with a bow before the Neb Lord of the World, Ausar.
- No longer to be confused with the Christmas present or package 'nicely wrapped' with a bow on top and placed under the Tree.
- We are the Tree, the Karest, the Presence that comes before the Awesome Presence, Ausar, Neb, Lord of the World.

Kemetic Karest mas Celebration & Education

W/Ausar & Imiut Symbol

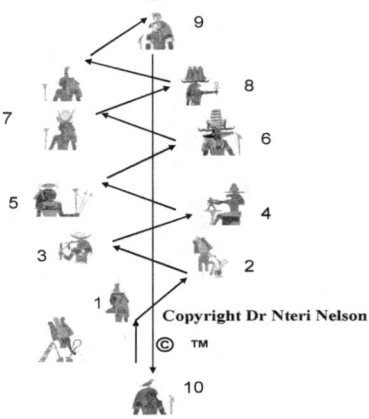

**Order of Adorning
Spheres of the Neteru
Lightening Flash of Re Ascension**

Bringing Heaven to Earth

- Step We undergo a Spiritual reconstruction
- Step We understand a truer meaning of the Resurrection of the Sun-Son/Daughter which we call Heru the Karest in our practice of a Kemetic Karest mas Celebration.

Duau, Duau, Duau
Neter Neteru

Kemetic Karest mas Celebration & Education

Sacred Symbols, Demystifying, Decoding, Disspelling, Revealing, Unveiling, Unshrouding, Connecting The Dots, Activating the 1st Eye, Panoply Seen, Lineage Understood, Ungarbling the Garbled, Greatness Revealed, Neteru Livingness, Neteru Resurrection

Afrikan Origins of The Ancient Wisdom

Step 10a What you will want to have on hand for your Celebration.
1. Tamarisk/Evergreen Tree & stand, white lights (purchase yourself)

Available at www.rrrk.net
2. Djed Pillar
3. Libation Cup
4. Neteru Spheres (bulbs)
5. Red and White Crown (Elders/Adults)
6. Red and White Crown (Children)
7. Laws of Maat Poster (large)
8. Laws of Maat Poster (small)
9. Re ascension into Sacredness Poster
10. Re ascension into Sacredness CD
11. Qualities & Image of the Neteru Poster (Large)
12. Qualities & Image of the Neteru Poster (small)
13. Hall of Amenta Going before the Shrine of Ausar Poster
14. Hymn to Heru Poster
15. Tamarisk/Djed Pillar Tree Poster
16. MerKaBa Light Body Poster
17. Recitation at each of the 4 Directions Poster
18. Scale
19. Feather of Maat upon the Scale/ Gift of
20. Cord/Rope

Kemetic Karest mas Celebration & Education

21. Amsu Heru 5- Pointed Star Top of Tree
The Academy of Kemetic Education & Wellness, Inc. thanks you for your support in utilizing the many services we provide to the community. Your support in the purchase of this book from our web site enables us to strengthen our Educational Institution building efforts for present and future generations. We thank you for telling friends, family, and community about this book and how to acquire their own copy by visiting ***www.rrrk.net***. I trust you will find the work at hand of personal value, but also take satisfaction in knowing that you are helping to educate the world about the tremendous contribution of Afrikan people to World Civilization.

Duau,
In the Spirit of Maat and the Law of Reciprocity

▲**Bibliography:**
Nelson, Nteri (Terri). (2011). *KaAbBa:The Great Pyramid is The Tree of Life:MerKaBa*. Mattapan, MA: Academy Kemetic Education & Wellness, Inc.
Nelson, Nteri (Terri). (2000). *KaAbBa Building The Lighted Temple*. Mattapan, MA: Academy of Kemetic Education & Wellness, Inc.
Nelson, Nteri (Terri). (2000). *Secrets of Race & Consciousness*. Mattapan, MA: Academy of Kemetic Education & Wellness, Inc.
Nelson, Nteri (Terri). (2008). *Ausar, The Pope, Santa Claus, Christmas and Christianity*. Mattapan, MA: Academy of Kemetic Education & Wellness, Inc.

Other Titles by Author:
Nelson, Nteri (Terri). (1999). *The Ausarian Dramatization of The Story of The Tree of Life Key*. Mattapan, MA: Academy of Kemetic Education
Nelson, Nteri (Terri). (2009). *Afrikan Cosmology of Kemet The Golden Sun Egg Uncracked. The NU'N' Word Negg ur The Goose Goddess Who Laid The Sun Egg, the Cosmic Egg*. Mattapan, MA: Academy of Kemetic Education & Wellness, Inc.
Nelson, Nteri (Terri). (1996). *On The Way To Finding Your Soulmate*. Mattapan, MA: Academy of Kemetic Education & Wellness, Inc.
Nelson, Nteri (Terri). (1998). *The Right Relation-ship Workbook*. Mattapan, MA: Academy of Kemetic Education & Wellness, Inc.

www.ingramcontent.com/pod-product-compliance
Lightning Source LLC
Chambersburg PA
CBHW050600300426
44112CB00013B/2002